Please return / renew by date shown.
You can renew at: **norlink.norfolk.gov.uk**
or by telephone: **0344 800 8006**
Please have your library card & PIN ready.

- - JAN 2013

- 9 APR 2014

STAG'S LEAP

STAG'S LEAP

Sharon Olds

CAPE POETRY

Published by Jonathan Cape 2012

2 4 6 8 10 9 7 5 3 1

Copyright © Sharon Olds 2012

First published in Great Britain in 2012 by
Jonathan Cape
Random House, 20 Vauxhall Bridge Road,
London SW1V 2SA

www.randomhouse.co.uk

Addresses for companies within The Random House Group Limited
can be found at: www.randomhouse.co.uk/offices.htm

The Random House Group Limited Reg. No. 954009

A CIP catalogue record for this book
is available from the British Library

ISBN 9780224096942

The Random House Group Limited supports The Forest Stewardship Council (FSC®),
the leading international forest certification organisation. Our books carrying the FSC
label are printed on FSC® certified paper. FSC is the only forest certification scheme
endorsed by the leading environmental organisations, including Greenpeace. Our paper
procurement policy can be found at www.randomhouse.co.uk/environment

MIX
Paper from
responsible sources
FSC
www.fsc.org   FSC® C016897

Typeset in Bembo by Palimpsest Book Production Limited
Falkrik, Stirlingshire

Printed and bound in Great Britain by
MPG Books Group Ltd, Bodmin, Cornwall

811 OLD

CONTENTS

January–December

While he told me, I looked from small thing
to small thing, in our room, the face
of the bedside clock, the sepia postcard
of a woman bending down to a lily.
Later, when we took off our clothes, I saw
his deep navel, and the cindery lichen
skin between the male breasts, and from
outside the shower curtain's terrible membrane
I called out something like flirting to him,
and he smiled. Before I turned out the light,
he touched my face, then turned away,
then the dark. Then every scene I thought of
I visited accompanied by a death-spirit,
everything was chilled with it,
each time I woke, I lay in dreading
bliss to feel and hear him sigh
and snore. Near sunrise, behind overcast, he got
up to go in and read on the couch,
as he often did,
and in a while I followed him,
as I often had,
and snoozed on him, while he read, and he laid
an arm across my back. When I opened
my eyes, I saw two tulips stretched
away from each other extreme in the old
vase with the grotto carved out of a hill
and a person in it, underground,
praying, my imagined shepherd in make-believe paradise.

UNSPEAKABLE

Now I come to look at love
in a new way, now that I know I'm not
standing in its light. I want to ask my
almost-no-longer husband what it's like to not
love, but he does not want to talk about it,
he wants a stillness at the end of it.
And sometimes I feel as if, already,
I am not here — to stand in his thirty-year
sight, and not in love's sight,
I feel an invisibility
like a neutron in a cloud chamber buried in a mile-long
accelerator, where what cannot
be seen is inferred by what the visible
does. After the alarm goes off,
I stroke him, my hand feels like a singer
who sings along him, as if it is
his flesh that's singing, in its full range,
tenor of the higher vertebrae,
baritone, bass, contrabass.
I want to say to him, now, What
was it like, to love me — when you looked at me,
what did you see? When he loved me, I looked
out at the world as if from inside
a profound dwelling, like a burrow, or a well, I'd gaze
up, at noon, and see Orion
shining — when I thought he loved me, when I thought
we were joined not just for breath's time,
but for the long continuance,
the hard candies of femur and stone,
the fastnesses. He shows no anger,
I show no anger but in flashes of humour,
all is courtesy and horror. And after

4

the first minute, when I say, Is this about
her, and he says, No, it's about
you, we do not speak of her.

THE FLURRY

When we talk about when to tell the kids,
we are so together, so concentrated.
I mutter, 'I feel like a killer.' '*I'm*
the killer' – taking my wrist – he says,
holding it. He is sitting on the couch,
the worn indigo chintz around him,
rich as a night tide, with jellies,
I am sitting on the floor. I look up at him
as if within some chamber of matedness,
some dust I carry around me. Tonight,
to breathe its Magellanic field is less
painful, maybe because he is drinking
a wine grown where I was born – fog,
eucalyptus, sempervirens – and I'm
sharing the glass with him. 'Don't catch
my cold,' he says, ' – oh that's right, you *want*
to catch my cold.' I should not have told him that,
I tell him I will try to fall out of
love with him, but I feel I will love him
all my life. He says he loves me
as the mother of our children, and new troupes
of tears mount to the acrobat platforms
of my ducts and do their burning leaps,
some of them jump straight sideways, and for a
moment, I imagine a flurry
of tears like a wirra of knives thrown
at a figure to outline it – a heart's spurt
of rage. It glitters, in my vision, I nod
to it, it is my hope.

MATERIAL ODE

O tulle, O taffeta, O grosgrain –
I call upon you now, girls,
of fabrics and the woman I sing. My husband
had said he was probably going to leave me – not
for sure, but likely, maybe – and no, it did not
have to do with her. O satin, O
sateen, O velvet, O fucking velveeta –
the day of the doctors' dress-up dance,
the annual folderol, the lace,
the net, he said it would be hard for her
to see me there, dancing with him,
would I mind not going. And since I'd been
for thirty years enarming him,
I enarmed him further – *Arma Virumque,*
sackcloth, ashen embroidery! As he
put on his tux, I saw his slight
smirk into the mirror, as he did his bow tie,
but after more than three decades, you have some
affection for each other's little faults,
and it suited me to cherish the belief
no meanness could happen between us. Fifty-
fifty we had made the marriage,
fifty-fifty its demise. And when he came
home and shed his skin, Reader,
I slept with him, thinking it meant
he was back, his body was speaking for him,
and as it spoke, its familiar sang
from the floor, the old-boy tie. O silk,
O slub, O cocoon stolen. It is something
our species does, isn't it,
we take what we can. Or else there'd be grubs
who kept people, in rooms, to produce
placentas for the larvae's use, there would be
a cow who would draw from our wombs our unborn

7

offspring, to make of them shoes for a calf.
O bunny-pyjamas of children! Love
where loved. O babies' flannel sleeper
with a slice of cherry pie on it.
Love only where loved! O newborn suit
with a smiling worm over the heart, it is
forbidden to love where we are not loved.

TELLING MY MOTHER

Outside her window, a cypress, under
the weight of the Pacific wind,
was bending luxuriously. To tell
my mother that my husband is leaving me . . .
I took her on a walk, taking her fleshless
hand like a passerine's claw, I bought her
a doughnut and a hairnet, I fed her. On the gnarled
magnolia, in the fog, the blossoms and buds were like
all the moons in one night – full,
gibbous, crescent. I'd practised the speech,
bringing her up toward the truth slowly,
preparing her. And the moment I told her,
she looked at me in shock and dismay.
But when will I ever see him again?!
she cried out. I held hands with her,
and steadied us, joking. Above her spruce, through the
coastal mist, for a moment, a small,
dry, sandy, glistering star. Then I
felt in my whole body, for a second,
that I have not loved enough – I could almost
see my husband's long shape,
wraithing up. I did not know him,
I did not work not to lose him, and I lost him,
and I've told my mother. And it's clear from her harrowed
sorrowing cheeks and childhood mountain-lake
eyes that she loves me. So the men are gone,
and I'm back with Mom. I always feared this would happen,
I thought it would be a pure horror,
but it's just home, Mom's house
and garden, earth, olive and willow,
beech, orchid, and the paperweight
dusted with opal, inside it the arms of a
nebula raking its heavens with a soft screaming.

SILENCE, WITH TWO TEXTS

When we lived together, the silence in the home
was denser than the silence would be
after he left. Before, the silence
was like a large commotion of industry
at a distance, like the downroar of mining. When he went,
I studied my once-husband's silence like an almost
holy thing, the call of a newborn born
mute. Text: 'Though its presence is detected
by the absence of what it negates, silence
possesses a power which presages fear
for those in its midst. Unseen, unheard,
unfathomable, silence dis-
concerts because it conceals.' Text:
'The waters compassed me about, even to
the soul: the depth closed me round
about, the weeds were wrapped about
my head.' I lived alongside him, in his hush
and reserve, sometimes I teased him, calling his
abstracted mask his Alligator Look,
seeking how to accept him as
he was, under the law that he could not
speak – and when I shrieked against the law
he shrinked down into its absolute,
he rose from its departure gate.
And he seemed almost like a hero, to me,
living, as I was, under the law
that I could not see the one I had chosen
but only consort with him as a being
fixed as an element, almost
ideal, no envy or meanness. In the last
weeks, by day we moved through the tearing
apart, along its length, of the union,
and by night silence lay down with blindness,
and sang, and saw.

GRAMERCY

The last time we slept together –
and then I can't remember when
it was, I used to be a clock
of sleeping together, and now it drifts,
in me, somewhere, the knowledge, in one of those
washes on maps of deserts, those spacious
wastes – the last time, he paused,
at some rest stop, some interval
between the unrollings, he put his palm
on my back, between the shoulder blades.
It was as if he were suing for peace,
asking if this could be over – maybe not
just this time, but over. He was solid
within me, suing for peace. And I
subsided, but then my bright tail
lolloped again, and I whispered, Just one
more?, and his indulgent grunt
seemed, to me, to have pleasure, and even
affection, in it – and my life, as it
was incorporated in flesh, was burst with the
sweet smashes again. And then
we lay and looked at each other – or I looked
at him, into his eyes. Maybe that
was the last time – not knowing
it was last, not solemn, yet that signal given,
that hand laid down on my back, not a gauntlet
but a formal petition for reprieve, a sign for Grant Mercy.

THE LAST HOUR

Suddenly, the last hour
before he took me to the airport, he stood up,
bumping the table, and took a step
toward me, and like a figure in an early
science fiction movie he leaned
forward and down, and opened an arm,
knocking my breast, and he tried to take some
hold of me, I stood and we stumbled,
and then we stood, around our core, his
hoarse cry of awe, at the centre,
at the end, of our life. Quickly, then,
the worst was over, I could comfort him,
holding his heart in place from the back
and smoothing it from the front, his own
life continuing, and what had
bound him, around his heart – and bound him
to me – now lying on and around us,
sea-water, rust, light, shards,
the little eternal curls of eros
beaten out straight.

LAST LOOK

In the last minute of our marriage, I looked into
his eyes. All that day until then, I had been
comforting him, for the shock he was in
at his pain – the act of leaving me
took him back, to his own early
losses. But now it was time to go beyond
comfort, to part. And his eyes seemed to me,
still, like the first ocean, wherein
the blue-green algae came into their early
language, his sea-wide iris still
essential, for me, with the depths in which
our firstborn, and then our second, had turned,
on the sides of their tongues the taste buds for the moon-bland
nectar of our milk – *our* milk. In his gaze,
rooms of the dead; halls of loss; fog-
emerald; driven, dirty-rice snow:
he was in there somewhere, I looked for him,
and he gave me the gift, he let me in,
knowing he would never once, in this world or in
any other, have to do it again,
and I saw him, not as he really was, I was
still without the strength of anger, but I
saw him see me, even now
that dropping down into trust's affection
in his gaze, and I held it, some seconds, quiet,
and I said, Good-bye, and he said, Good-bye,
and I closed my eyes, and rose up out of the
passenger seat in a spiral like someone
coming up out of a car gone off a
bridge into deep water. And two and
three Septembers later, and even
the September after that, that September in New York,
I was glad I had looked at him. And when I
told a friend how glad I'd been,

she said, *Maybe it's like with the families*
of the dead, even the families of those
who died in the Towers — that need to see
the body, no longer inhabited
by what made them the one we loved — somehow
it helps to say good-bye to the actual,

and I saw, again, how blessed my life has been,
first, to have been able to love,
then, to have the parting now behind me,
and not to have lost him when the kids were young,
and the kids now not at all to have lost him,
and not to have lost him when he loved me, and not to have
lost someone who could have loved me for life.

Then the drawing on the label of our favourite red wine
looks like my husband, casting himself off a
cliff in his fervour to get free of me.
His fur is rough and cosy, his face
placid, tranced, ruminant,
the bough of each furculum reaches back
to his haunches, each tine of it grows straight up
and branches, like a model of his brain, archaic,
unwieldy. He bears its bony tray
level as he soars from the precipice edge,
dreamy. When anyone escapes, my heart
leaps up. Even when it's I who am escaped from,
I am half on the side of the leaver. It's so quiet,
and empty, when he's left. I feel like a landscape,
a ground without a figure. *Sauve*
qui peut – let those who can save themselves
save themselves. Once I saw a drypoint of someone
tiny being crucified
on a fallow deer's antlers. I feel like his victim,
and he seems my victim, I worry that the outstretched
legs on the hart are bent the wrong way as he
throws himself off. Oh my mate. I was vain of his
faithfulness, as if it was
a compliment, rather than a state
of partial sleep. And when I wrote about him, did he
feel he had to walk around
carrying my books on his head like a stack of
posture volumes, or the rack of horns
hung where a hunter washes the venison
down with the sauvignon? Oh leap,
leap! Careful of the rocks! Does the old
vow have to wish him happiness
in his new life, even sexual
joy? I fear so, at first, when I still

can't tell us apart. Below his shaggy
belly, in the distance, lie the even dots
of a vineyard, its vines not blasted, its roots
clean, its bottles growing at the ends of their
blowpipes as dark, green, wavering groans.

KNOWN TO BE LEFT

If I pass a mirror, I turn away,
I do not want to look at her,
and she does not want to be seen. Sometimes
I don't see exactly how to go on doing this.
Often, when I feel that way,
within a few minutes I am crying, remembering
his body, or an area of it,
his backside often, a part of him
just right now to think of, luscious, not too
detailed, and his back turned to me.
After tears, the chest is less sore,
as if some goddess of humanness
within us has caressed us with a gush of tenderness.
I guess that's how people go on, without
knowing how. I am so ashamed
before my friends – to be known to be left
by the one who supposedly knew me best,
each hour is a room of shame, and I am
swimming, swimming, holding my head up,
smiling, joking, ashamed, ashamed,
like being naked with the clothed, or being
a child, having to try to behave
while hating the terms of your life. In me now
there's a being of sheer hate, like an angel
of hate. On the badminton lawn, she got
her one shot, pure as an arrow,
while through the eyelets of my blouse the no-see-ums
bit the flesh no one seems now
to care to touch. In the mirror, the torso
looks like a pinup hives martyr,
or a cream pitcher speckled with henbit and pussy-paws,
full of the milk of human kindness
and unkindness, and no one is lining up to drink.
But look! I am starting to give him up!

17

I believe he is not coming back. Something
has died, inside me, believing that,
like the death of a crone in one twin bed
as a child is born in the other. Have faith,
old heart. What is living, anyway,
but dying.

OBJECT LOSS

The banjo clock, suspended in thirty-weight
dreaming marriedness, for thirty
years, doesn't come down easy from the wall,
rusted to the hook, then it lurches up,
its gangle throat glugs. Big-headed, murmurous,
in my arms it's like a diver's bell,
Davy-Jonesed. When I lean it by the back
door, it tocks, and ticks, it doesn't even
cross my mind I might wish to kick it.
Using his list, I remove his family
furnishings, the steeple clock,
the writing-arm chair, the tole-and-brass
drawing table – I had not known
how connected I'd felt, through him, to a world of
handed-down, signed, dated,
appraised things, pedigreed matter.
As I add to the stash which will go to him,
I feel as if I'm falling away
from family – as if each ponderous
object had been keeping me afloat. No, they were
the scenery of the play now closing,
lengthy run it had. My pitchfork
tilts against the wall in the dining room,
web thick in its tines, spider
dangling in one cul-de-sac . . .
What if loss can be without
dishonour. His harpoon – a Beothuk harpoon –
and its bone and sinew and tusk and brine-wood
creel I add to the pile, I render
unto Caesar, and my shame is winter sunlight
on a pine floor, and it moves, it sways like an old dancer.

POEM FOR THE BREASTS

Like other identical twins, they can be
better told apart in adulthood.
One is fast to wrinkle her brow,
her brain, her quick intelligence. The other
dreams inside a constellation,
freckles of Orion. They were born when I was thirteen,
they rose up, half out of my chest,
now they're forty, wise, generous.
I am inside them – in a way, under them,
or I carry them, I'd been alive so many years without them.
I can't say I am them, though their feelings are almost
my feelings, as with someone one loves. They seem,
to me, like a gift that I have to give.
That boys were said to worship their category of
being, almost starve for it,
did not escape me, and some young men
loved them the way one would want, oneself, to be loved.
All year they have been calling to my departed husband,
singing to him, like a pair of soaking
sirens on a scaled rock.
They can't believe he's left them, it's not in their
vocabulary, they being made
of promise – they're like literally kept vows.
Sometimes, now, I hold them a moment,
one in each hand, twin widows,
heavy with grief. They were a gift to me,
and then they were ours, like thirsty nurslings
of excitement and plenty. And now it's the same
season again, the very week
he moved out. Didn't he whisper to them,
Wait here for me one year? No.
He said, God be with you, God
by with you, God-bye, for the rest

of this life and for the long nothing. And they do not
know language, they are waiting for him, my
Christ they are dumb, they do not even
know they are mortal – sweet, I guess,
refreshing to live with, beings without
the knowledge of death, creatures of ignorant suffering.

Winter

NOT GOING TO HIM

Minute by minute, I do not get up and just
go to him –
by day, twenty blocks away;
by night, due across the city's
woods where night-crowned heron sleep.
It is what I do now: not go, not
see or touch. And after eleven
million six hundred sixty-four thousand
minutes of not, I am a stunned knower
of not. Then I let myself picture him
a moment: the bone that seemed to surface in his
wrist after I had held my father's
hand in coma; then up, over
his arm, with its fold, from which for a friend
he gave his blood. Then a sense of his presence
returns, his flesh which seemed, to me,
made as if before the Christian
God existed, a north-island baby's
body become a man's, with that pent
spirit, its heels dug in, those time-worn
heels, those elegant flat feet;
and then, in a sweep, calf shin knee thigh pelvis
waist, and I run my irises
over his feathered chest, and on his neck,
the scar, dollhouse saucer of tarnish
set in time's throat, and up to the nape and then
dive again, as the swallows fly
at speed – cliff and barn and bank
and tree – at twilight, just over the surface
of a sloping terrain. He is alive, he breathes
and moves! My body may never learn
not to yearn for that one, or this could be
a first farewell to him, a life-do-us-part.

PAIN I DID NOT

When my husband left, there was pain I did not
feel, which those who lose the one
who loves them feel. I was not driven
against the grate of a mortal life, but
just the slowly shut gate
of preference. At times I envied them –
what I saw as the honourable suffering
of one who is thrown against that iron
grille. I think he had come, in private, to
feel he was dying, with me, and if
he had what it took to rip his way out, with his
teeth, then he could be born. And so he went
into another world – this
world, where I do not see or hear him –
and my job is to eat the whole car
of my anger, part by part, some parts
ground down to steel-dust. I like best
the cloth seats, blue-grey, first
car we bought together, long since
marked with the scrubbed stains – drool,
tears, ice cream, no wounds, but only
the month's blood of release, and the letting
go when the water broke.

THE WORST THING

One side of the highway, the waterless hills.
The other, in the distance, the tidal wastes,
estuaries, bay, throat
of the ocean. I had not put it into
words, yet – the worst thing,
but I thought that I could say it, if I said it
word by word. My friend was driving,
sea-level, coastal hills, valley,
foothills, mountains – the slope, for both,
of our earliest years. I had been saying
that it hardly mattered to me now, the pain,
what I minded was – say there was
a god – of love – and I'd given – I had meant
to give – my life – to it – and I
had failed, well I could just suffer for that –
but what, if I,
had harmed, love? I howled this out,
and on my glasses the salt water pooled, almost
sweet to me, then, because it was named,
the worst thing – and once it was named,
I knew there was no god, there were only
people. And my friend reached over,
to where my fists clutched each other,
and the back of his hand rubbed them, a second,
with clumsiness, with the courtesy
of no eros, the homemade kindness.

Sometimes, now, I think of the back
of his head as a physiognomy,
blunt, rich as if with facial hair,
the convex stonewall shapes of the skull
like brow nose cheeks, as hard to read
as surfaces of the earth. He was as
mysterious to me as that phrenology –
occiput, lamboid – but known like a home
outcrop of rock, and his quiet had
the truthfulness, for me, of something
older than the human. I knew and did not
know his brain, and its woody mountain
casing, but the sheer familiarness
of his brow was like a kind of knowledge,
I had my favourite pores on its skin,
and the chaos, multiplicity, and
generousness of them was like
the massy stars over the desert.
He hardly ever frowned, he seemed
serene, as if above or alien
to anger. Now, I can see that his eyes
were sometimes bleak or sullen, but I saw them
as lakes – one could sound them, and receive
no sense of their bounds or beds. Something in
the paucity of his cheeks, the sunken
cheekbones, always touched me. Bold
Old English cartilage of the nose, wide
eloquent curve of the archer's bow, its
quiver sometimes empty as if languagelessness
was a step up, in evolution,
from the chatter of consciousness. Now
that I travel the land of his sealed mask
of self in memory, again, touching
his contours, as if I am the singing blind,

I feel that ignorant love gave me
a life. But from within my illusion of him
I could not see him, or know him. I did not
have the art or there's no art
to find the mind's construction in the face:
he was a gentleman on whom I built
an absolute trust.

Slowly fitting my pinkie tip down
into the feral eggshell fallen
from inside the chimney, I lift it up
close to my eye, the coracle dome
hung with ashes, rivered with flicks
of chint, robes of the unknown – only
a sojourner, in our home, where the heart,
after its long, good years,
was sparrow-netted to make its own
cage, jessed with its jesses, limed
with its radiant lime. And above the tiny
tossed-off cloak of the swift, in the back
reaches of the Puritan oven, on a bed
of sprung traps, the mice in them
long gone to meltdown and to maggotmeal
and to wet dust and dry dust
there lies another topped shell –
next to it, its doffed skull
tressed with spinneret sludge, speckled with
flue-mash flecks, or the morse of a species –
when I lift it up, its yolk drops out, hard
amber, light coming through it, fringed
in a tonsure of mold and soot. If I ever
prayed, as a child, for everlasting
union, these were its shoes: one dew-licked
kicked-off slipper of a being now flying, one
sunrise-milk-green boot of the dead,
which I wore, as I dreamed.

LOVE

I had thought it was something we were in. I had thought we
    were
in it that day, in the capital
of his early province – how could we
have not been in it, in our hotel bed, in the
cries through the green grass-blade. Then,
knees weak, I thought I was in it when I said
would he mind going out into the town on his own.
I knew there was sorrow there, byways, worn
scrimshaw of a child's isolateness.
And who had pulled us down on the bed for the
second time that day, who had
given-taken the kiss that would not
stop till the cry – it was I, sir, it was I,
my lady, but I thought that all we did
was done in love's sight. So he went out by himself
into the boyhood place of deaths
and icy waters, and I lay in that bowl-of-
cream bed purring. The room was like the bridge of a
ship, windows angled out over the harbour –
through thick, smooth Greenland glass I
saw the port city, I curled and sinuous'd
and slow-flicked my most happy tail, and
farther into cold fog
I let him go, I lay and stretched on love's
fucking stretcher, and let him wander on his
own the haunt salt mazes. I thought
wherever we were, we were in lasting love –
even in our separateness and
loneliness, in love – even the
iceberg just outside the mouth, its
pallid, tilting, jade-white
was love's, as we were. We had said so. And its inner
cleavings went translucent and opaque,

violet and golden, as the afternoon passed, and there were
feathers of birds inside it preserved, and
nest-down and maybe a bootlace, even
a tern half shell, a baby shoe, love's
tiny dory as if permanent
inside the bright overcast.

THE HEALERS

When they say, *If there are any doctors aboard,*
would they make themselves known, I remember when my then
husband would rise, and I would get to be
the one he rose from beside. They say now
that it does not work, unless you are equal.
And after those first thirty years,
I was not the one he wanted to rise from
or return to – not I but she who would also
rise, when such were needed. Now I see them,
lifting, side by side, on wide,
medical, wading-bird wings – like storks with the
doctor bags of like-loves-like
dangling from their beaks. Oh well. It was the way
it was, he did not feel happy when words
were called for, and I stood.

Hoddley, Poddley, Puddles and Fogs,
Cats are to Marry the Poodle Dogs;
Cats in Blue Jackets and Dogs in Red Hats,
What Will Become of the Mice and Rats?
    Had a trust fund, had a thief in,
    Had a husband, could not keep him.
Fiddle-Dee-Dee, Fiddle-Dee-Dee,
The Fly Has Left the Humble-Bee.
They Went to the Court, and Unmarried Was She:
The Fly Has Left the Humble-Bee.
    Had a sow twin, had a reap twin,
    Had a husband, could not keep him.
In Marble Halls as White as Milk,
Lined with a Skin as Soft as Silk,
Within a Fountain Crystal-Clear,
A Golden Apple Doth Appear.
No Doors There Are to This Stronghold
Yet Robbers Break In and Steal the Gold.
    Had an egg cow, had a cream hen,
    Had a husband, could not keep him.
Formed Long Ago, Yet Made Today,
Employed While Others Sleep;
What Few Would Like to Give Away,
Nor Any Wish to Keep.
    Had a nap man, had a neap man,
    Had a flood man, could not keep him.
Ickle, Ockle, Blue Bockle,
Fishes in the Sea.
If You Want a Left Wife,
Please Choose Me.
    Had a safe of 4X sheepskin,
    Had a brook brother, could not keep him.
Inter, Mitzy, Titzy, Tool,
Ira, Dura, Dominee,

Oker, Poker, Dominocker,
Out Goes Me.
    Had a lamb, slung in keepskin,
    Had some ewe-milk, in it seethed him.
There Was an Old Woman Called Nothing-at-All,
Who Lived in a Dwelling Exceedingly Small;
A Man Stretched His Mouth to the Utmost Extent,
And Down at One Gulp House and Old Woman Went.
    Had a rich pen, had a cheap pen,
    Had a husband, could not keep him.
Put him in this nursery shell,
And here you keep him very well.

SOMETHING THAT KEEPS

Heavy on the cupboard the wreath hangs,
the bulbs pouring up their hull withers.
Borne home, from the garlic farm,
it will last a year, she says, not
like one from Lucky's, which could sprout, or rattle –
they sell the previous season's, she says,
they think of it as something that keeps.
One thing I did not think
I had to worry about was that
my then husband or I would be willing
that the spirit of the other be taken apart.
Meanwhile, I left minutes of each hour,
hours of each day, days of each week,
untended – to the whim of mildew, stallor,
and the lonesome tooth of the granary scuttler.
Girdle of curdled pubic roots,
lumped breasts, husk-spouted nipples,
eyeballs with iris gone bazook medusa,
I thought that he and I were in
some sacred precinct – which does not exist,
we were in the barn, the store, the bin,
the pan, the bowl, the breath. One two three
four five six seven eight nine ten eleven
thirty-two heads on the succulent throstle.
It is in the past, enough looking back,
it is gone, it is more over with
than the shocks of childhood. Rope of heaven,
ladder of hex, all is in
the tending, and we cannot tend
another's rows. But I did not tend
my knowledge of who he was – nor did he
his of me, nor did he care to.
Braiding of summer, harvest, winter,
moonlight, noon, frost, enough,

lie quiet on the wall that guards the dishes,
honour the clove now gone to ash,
the clove once split at its core by the liquid shoot.

THE EASEL

When I build a fire, I feel purposeful –
proud I can unscrew the wing nuts
from off the rusted bolts, dis-
assembling one of the things my ex
left when he left right left. And laying its
narrow, polished, maple angles
across the kindling, providing for updraft –
good. Then by flame-light I see: I am burning
his med-school easel. How can that be,
after the hours and hours – all told, maybe
weeks, a month of stillness – modelling
for him, our first years together,
odour of acrylic, stretch of treated
canvas. I am burning his left-behind craft,
he who was the first to turn
our family, naked, into art.
What if someone had told me, thirty
years ago: If you give up, now,
wanting to be an artist, he might
love you all your life – what would I
have said? I didn't even have an art,
it would come from out of our family's life –
what could I have said: nothing will stop me.

So much had become so connected to him
that it seemed to belong to him, so that now,
flying, for hours, above the Atlantic
still felt like being over his realm.
And then, in the distance, a sort of land —
rows and rows of tilted, ruched-back
pyramids and fangs of snow —
appeared, and along its bitten hems, in the
water, hundreds of giant, white
beings, or rafts, nuzzled the shore,
moon-calves, stoats, dories, ships,
tankers green-shadowed cream, a family
of blossom-tree icebergs, his familiars — never
mine, but once contiguous
to what I felt was almost mine,
they were like the flowers a boreal storybook
king would give his queen, hoarfrost
lilies. It struck cold awe to my heart,
now, to look at who I had been
who had thought it was impossible
that he or I could touch another.
Tu wit, tu woo — lhude sing
goddamn, cuckoo, to look back
and see myself living, vowblind, in cloud
cuckold land. The glacierscape called it
up, the silent, shining tulle,
the dreaming hats and cubes, the theorems
and corollaries, that girl who had thought
a wedding promise was binding as a law
of physics. Now, I stood outside
the kingdoms, phyla, orders, genera,
the turquoise-sided frozen plenty,
as if, when he took his stones and went home, he took
snow, and ice, and glaciers, and shores,

and the sea, and the northern hemisphere,
half of the great blue-and-white aggie
itself, I sat on the air above it
and looked down on its uninhabitable beauty.

Spring

ONCE IN A WHILE I GAVE UP

Once in a while, I gave up, and let myself
remember how much I'd liked the way my ex's
hips were set, the head of the femur which
rode, not shallow, not deep, in the socket
of the pelvis, wrapped in the iliofemoral and
ischiofemoral ligaments,
the ball bearings suspended just so
to give him that walk. Wooden yokes, in
grade-school foreign-country-custom
movies, had moved like that, over opulent
zinc buckets of milk – the motion
was authentic, it was from another place, it was
planetary, it was model-of-the-solar-
systemic. I idolised it without
reserve, caution, or limit, I adored it with an
unprotected joy. Months,
a year later, I still dreamed it
sometimes, the illusion of a constellation
visible only from a certain vantage,
glittering peaks of his iliac crest:
A is to B up, as B is to
C across, as C is to D
down, bright winching bitings, I even
let my right hand describe
the curve of that posterior, cool
thirty-year night's waxing gibbous
now set – in stubborn fundamentalist
conviction my hand described the mortal crescent.

TO OUR MISCARRIED ONE, AGE THIRTY NOW

Though I never saw you, only your clouds,
I was afraid of you, of how you differed
from what we had wanted you to be. And it's as if
you waited, then, where such waiting is done,
for when I would look beside me – and here
you are, in the world of forms, where my wifehood
is now, and every action with him,
as if a thousand years from now
you and I are in some antechamber
where the difference between us is of little matter,
you with perhaps not much of a head yet,
dear garden one, you among the shovels
and spades and wafts of beekeeper's shroud
and sky-blue kidskin gloves.
That he left me is not much, compared
to your leaving the earth – your shifting places
on it, and shifting shapes – you threw off your
working clothes of arms and legs,
and moved house, from uterus
to toilet bowl and jointed stem
and sewer out to float the rivers and
bays in painless pieces. And yet
the idea of you has come back to where
I could see you today as a small, impromptu
god of the partial. When I leave for good,
would you hold me in your blue mitt
for the departure hence. I never thought
to see you again, I never thought to seek you.

FRENCH BRA

Then low in a fancy shop window, near my
anklebone, like a Hermes heel-wing
fitted with struts and ailerons,
fragile as a silk biplane, the *soutien-
gorge* lies, lissome, uncharged,
slack as a snakeskin husk. I stop,
I howl in seventh-grade French. The cups are
lace net, intricate as curtains in a
bee's house, in a kitchen where honey's
on the stove, in the mouth, in the pants – and there are pants,
in eyelet appliqué, and there are gold
pinions like brushes of touch along the tops of the
poitrine – and it's as if my body has not
heard, or hasn't believed, the news,
it wants to go in there and pick up those wisps,
those hippolyta harnesses, on its pinkie,
and bring them home to my ex and me,
mon ancien mari et moi. It's as if
I'd been in a club, with him, with secret
handshakes, and secret looks, and touches,
and *charmeuse* was in the club with us, and
ribbon, they were our wing'd attendants –
and satin, and dotted swiss, they were our
language, our food and furniture,
our garden and transportation and philosophy
and church, stateless state and deathless
death, our music and war. Everyone
dies. Sometimes a beloved dies,
and sometimes love. Such far worse happens,
this seems it should be a toy lament,
a doll's dressmaker's dummy's song,
though people are often murdered, to celebrate

the death of love. I stand, for a moment,
looking down, at the empty costumes
of luxury, the lingerie ghosts of my sojourn.

MY SON'S FATHER'S SMILE

In my sleep, our son, as a child, said,
of his father, *he smiled me* – as if into
existence, into the family built around the
young lives which had come from the charged
bouquets, the dense oasis. That smile,
those years, well what can a body say, I have
been in the absolute present of a fragrant
ignorance. And to live in those rooms,
where one of his smiles might emerge, like something
almost from another place,
another time, another set
of creatures, was to feel blessed, and to be
held in mysteriousness, and a little
in mourning. The thinness of his lips gave it
a simplicity, like a child's drawing
of a smile – a footbridge, turned over on its back, or seen
under itself, in water – and the archer's
bow gave it a curved unerring
symmetry, a shot to the heart. I look back on that un-
clouded face yet built of cloud,
and that waning crescent moon, that look
of deep, almost sad, contentment, and know myself
lucky, that I had out the whole
night of a half-life in that archaic
hammock, in a sky whose darkness is fading, that
first dream, from which I am now waking.

NOT QUIET ENOUGH

Dread and sorrow reaching, in time, into
every reach, there comes the hour
I wonder if my husband left me
because I was not quiet enough
in our bed. I can hardly see those nights
and afternoons, anymore, those mornings,
but now, for a moment, I can almost hear
the sound of him then, as if startled, or nearly
caught up with, nearly in the grip of something, then those
honeysuckle moans, trellis
and lattice to mine, in the body's mouth-
to-mouth full-out duet. He lived
so enclosed in himself, he seemed alive not
exactly like others, but hibernating –
I called for him through solid earth
until he woke, and left. Christ if my
cries woke him. Sometimes they were only
low, drenched, lock-clicks of the breath
stopped, then drifting in mortise-light
with him ... 11,000 nights,
he seemed content with me, he seemed to like
anything, any screak or high C, but were there
brayings that graded through off-key shimmer into
prism of bruise-colour, were there
mortal laments, mammal shrieks against
division, as if, in sex, we practise
the cauter of being parted. Or maybe
it was not my chirps, not the sounding
flesh of those sheets, floor, chairs, back
porches, a hayloft, woods, but this telling
of them – did his spirit turn against the spirit which
tolled our private, wild bell
from the public rooftop, I who had no other
gift to give the world but to hold what I

thought was love's mirror up to us –
ah now, no puff of mist on it.
After that life in the singing dream,
I woke, and feared he felt he was the human
sleeper, and I the glittering panther
holding him down, and screaming.

Summer

SEA-LEVEL ELEGY

Then my mind goes back to the summer rental,
the stairs down into the earth – I descend them
and turn, and pass the washing machine, and go
into the bedroom, one wall the solid
pane the warbler flew into skull-first,
the opposite wall the inches-thick
seagoing mirror. Even now,
I see us, long horizontals
in the luminous pool of the wall, speckled
by the silt of the old plate glass, spotted
like other animals. Above us are the pine
planks, planed, and sawn aslant,
and marked with the boot-sole ridges of the builders'
Timberlands. And there, behind the pillows, are the
alcoves in which the owners kept lasts
of shoes, like wooden feet, Petrarchan
ankle slippers, out from the toe
the last-tip sprouting – how many times, as if
risen from inside the earth, where I'd seemed to have
ocean-fathoms-flown, with him,
scarcely recognising, my gaze would
travel over the hermetic shapes of the
dummies shoemakers had shod. And I had clothed him
with my body and been clothed with him, again,
again, unquestioned, not fully seen,
not wanting to fully see. And now,
the image of him has gone inside
the raw closet, the naked bulb's
blazing golden pear beside his
August-island shaggy head.
That's it. Once, each summer, I howl,
and draw myself back, out of there, where
desire and joy, where ignorance, where

touch and the ideal, where unwilled yet wilful
blindness – once a year, I have mercy,
I let myself go down where I have lived, and then,
hand over hand, I pull myself back up.

When a caught mouse corpse lay hidden, for a week,
and stuck to the floor, I started setting
the traps on a few of our wedding china
floral salad plates. Late
one night when one has sprung, I put it on the
porch, to take it to the woods in the morning, but by
morning I forget, and by noon – and by after-
noon the Blue Willow's like a charnel roof
in Persia when the bodies of the dead were put for the
scholar vultures to pick the text
of matter and the text of spirit apart.
The mouse has become a furry barrow
burrowed into by a beetle striped
in stripes of hot and stripes of cold
coal – headfirst, it eats its way into
the stomach smoother than dirt, the mouse-bowels
saltier, beeswax and soap
stopped in the small intestinal channels.
And bugs little as seeds are seething
all over the hair, as if the rodent
were food rejoicing. And the *Nicrophorus*
cuts and thrusts, it rocks and rolls
its tomentose muzzle, and its wide shoulders,
in. And I know, I know, I should put
my dead marriage out on the porch
in the sun, and let who can, come
and nourish of it – change it, carry it
back to what it was assembled from,
back to the source of the light whereby it shone.

And had it been a year since I had stood,
looking down, into the Whirlpool
in the laundry nook of our August rental, not
sure what I was seeing – it looked like a woman
brought up in a net with fish. It was
a miniature woman, in a bathing suit,
lying back after the spin cycle –
the photograph of a woman, slightly
shaped over the contours of a damp towel.
I drew it out – radiant square
from some other world – maybe the daughter
of the elderly owners. And yet it looked like
someone we knew – I said, to my husband,
This was in with the sheets and towels.
Good heavens, he said. Where?! In
with the sheets and your running shorts. Doesn't it
look like your colleague? We gazed at the smile
and the older shapely body in its gleaming
rainbow sheath – surprise trout
of wash-day. An hour later, he found me,
and told me she had given him the picture
the day that they went running together
when I was away, he must have slipped it in
his pocket, he was so shocked to see it
again, he did not know what to say.
In a novel, I said, this would be when
the wife should worry – is there even the slightest
reason to worry. He smiled at me,
and took my hand, and turned to me,
and said, it seemed not by rote,
but as if it were a physical law
of the earth, I love you. And we made love,
and I felt so close to him – I had not
known he knew how to lie, and his telling me

touched my heart. Just once, later
in the day, I felt a touch seasick, as if
a deck were tilting under me –
a run he'd taken, not mentioned to me,
a fisher of men in the washing machine.
Just for a few minutes I had felt a little nervous.

ATTEMPTED BANQUET

Lugging of shellfish in coolers, boiling
and bouillabaissing – summer luncheon
we had tried to give, cancelling twice
when the parasite had come back to my gut,
then trying again, recurrent hope
of serving up the creatures of the shallow
deep. We joked about putting it off, but
underneath the joking, grim
and hidden, he wanted to leave me, and was
working toward it and against it, maybe worried
he could not do it, longing for it
and fearing it, and not speaking of it, bent
over the shucked crustaceans and the finny
wanderers from the tide pools, their feelers which
had writhed their last in the home language.
It touches with a sharp, shelling touch,
still, to remember his joyless labour
in the heat, we sweated side by side three
times like a spell or a curse, until,
on Labor Day, the salmon at last
undulated out the kitchen door in its
half-slip of thin cucumber scales
on its fluted platter to the table laid with a
linen cloth under the old
trees of life. And almost no one
actually got there, at the last minute there were
sprains and flus and in-laws and flats
so the few of us there moved through the heavy
air like kids at an empty school on a holiday,
and the wasted food was like some kind of
carnage. We lived on it a week, as we'd been
living, without my seeing it,
on the broken habit of what was not lasting
love. When I remember him

at the stove, the sight pierces me
with tenderness, he was suffering, then,
as I would soon. When I see that day,
at moments I see it almost without guilt,
or with a pure, shared guilt,
or a shared cause, without fault, and there is
nothing to be done for it,
it can only be known and borne, it cannot be
turned into anything fruitful or sweet,
but just be faced, as what it was,
just be eaten, portion of flesh and salt.

Fall

THE HAIRCUT

Then against my will I thought of the day he'd been
sick, and I'd cut my then husband's hair
to cheer him up. First I combed it,
sensing, with its teeth, the follicles
of his scalp. His hair was stiff from fever, close-
laid and flat, each plane a worn
conveyor belt come out of his head,
and his skull was flattish in back, with a hollow
in the centre. I loved to eat–eat–eat
with the scissors, to chew sheaf. He was
so tall it was like tree husbandry,
childish joy of tiptoe. On his shoulders,
the little bundles would accumulate,
like a medieval painting's kindling
dropped when a meteor passed over. He was so
handsome it was kind of adorable when he
looked horrible. His face that hour was
gaunt, the runnels of his cheeks concave, his
lower eyelids and the sacks below them
ogre-swollen, but within the rims
were the deep-sea swimmers of his eyes, the sounders,
by which I read the depth of his character, not
knowing how else but by beauty to read it,
and he closed them, he bowed, I did his nape
and patted up chaff from the floor. Before sleep,
I stroked his satiny hair, the viral
sweat creaming out at its edge, I petted his
coat and he took a handful of my hair in his
fist and gripped it. Don't be sick,
I said, OK, he said, and love
seemed to rest, on us, in a place
where, for that hour, it felt death could not

reach, and someone was singing, in my hearing, without
words, that no one can live without reaching
death, but I could have lived without having
loved almost without reserve, and for a
moment, then, I thought I lived forever with him.

CRAZY

I've said that he and I had been crazy
for each other, but maybe my ex and I were not
crazy for each other. Maybe we
were sane for each other, as if our desire
was almost not even personal –
it was personal, but that hardly mattered, since there
seemed to be no other woman
or man in the world. Maybe it was
an arranged marriage, air and water and
earth had planned us for each other – and fire,
a fire of pleasure like a violence
of kindness. To enter those vaults together, like a
solemn or laughing couple in formal
step or writhing hair and cry, seemed to
me like the earth's and moon's paths,
inevitable, and even, in a way,
shy – enclosed in a shyness together,
equal in it. But maybe I
was crazy about him – it is true that I saw
that light around his head when I'd arrive second
at a restaurant – oh for God's sake,
I was besotted with him. Meanwhile the planets
orbited each other, the morning and the evening
came. And maybe what he had for me
was unconditional, temporary
affection and trust, without romance,
though with fondness – with mortal fondness. There was no
tragedy, for us, there was
the slow-revealed comedy
of ideal and error. What precision of action
it had taken, for the bodies to hurtle through
the sky for so long without harming each other.

DISCANDIED

When my hand is groping on the toolroom shelf for ex-
marital liquor to drink by myself,
it bumps something it knows by one bump
and rustle, one chocolate bar, with almonds, then
the muffled thunk of another – he would hide them,
then give me one when I was sad. When he left,
he did not think, as who would,
to go to the caches and empty them, to the
traps and spring them. I take the fascia
of bars to the compost, denude them of their peel,
and chuck them in with the rumps and grinds,
the grounds and eden rinds,
and I carry the bowl outside, to the heap,
and trowel a pit in some eggshell crunch where the
potato sends its crisp shoots
of rage up, I tuck the cocoa
shards in – vanillin to vanillin,
very nut to very nut,
and remember how he hated it
when I tried to get him to talk to me,
tried with a certain steadiness –
nagged him to reveal himself –
maybe these desserts were not only gifts,
but bribes or stops, to close my mouth
an hour on sweetness.

BRUISE GHAZAL

Now a black-and-blue oval on my hip has turned blue-
violet as the ink-brand on the husk-fat of a prime
cut, sore as a lovebite, but too
large for a human mouth. I like it, my
flesh brooch – gold rim, envy-colour
cameo within, and violet mottle
on which the door-handle that bit is a black
purple with wiggles like trembling decapede
legs. I count back the days, and forward
to when it will go its rot colours and then
slowly fade. Some people think I should
be over my ex by now – maybe
I thought I might have been over him more
by now. Maybe I'm half over who he
was, but not who I thought he was, and not
over the wound, sudden deathblow
as if out of nowhere, though it came from the core
of our life together. Sleep now, Sharon,
sleep. Even as we speak, the work is being
done, within. You were born to heal.
Sleep and dream – but not of his return.
Since it cannot harm him, wound him, in your dream.

Years Later

ON READING A NEWSPAPER FOR THE
FIRST TIME AS AN ADULT

By evening, I am down to the last,
almost weightless, mineral-odoured
pages of the morning paper, and as I am
letting fall what I have read,
and creasing what's left lengthwise, the crackly
rustle and the feathery grease remind me that
what I am doing is what my then husband
did, that sitting waltz with the paper,
undressing its layers, blowsing it,
opening and closing its delicate bellows,
folding till only a single column is un-
taken in, a bone of print then
gnawed from the top down, until
the layers of the paper-wasp nest lay around him by the
couch in a greyish speckle dishevel. I left him to it,
the closest I wanted to get to the news was to
start to sleep with him, slowly, while he was
reading, the clouds of printed words
gradually becoming bedsheets around us.
When he left me, I thought, *If only I had read
the paper,* and vowed, *In two years,
I will have the Times delivered,* so here
I am, leaning back on the couch, in the smell of ink's
oil, its molecules like chipped bits of
ammonites suspended in shale,
lead's dust silvering me.
I have a finger, now, in the pie –
count me as a reader of the earth's gossip.
I weep to feel how I love to be like
my guy. I taste what he tastes each morning
without moving my lips.

MARITIME

Some mornings, the hem of the forewash had been almost
golden, alaskas and berings of foam
pulled along the tensile casing.
Often the surface was a ship's grey,
a destroyer's, flecks of sun, jellies,
sea stars, blood stars, men and women of war,
weed Venus hair. A month a year,
for thirty years. Nine hundred mornings,
sometimes we could tell, from the beach,
while taking our clothes off, how cold the water
was, by looking at it – and then,
at its icy touch, the nipples took
their barnacle glitter, underwater
a soft frigor bathed the sex as if
drawing her detailed outline in the seeing
brain, and he braced his knees in the press
of the swell, and I dove under, and near the
floor of this life I glided between his ankles, not
knowing, until he was behind me, if I had got
through without brushing them. Then,
the getting out, rising, half-poached
egg coming up out of its shell and membrane,
weight of the breasts finding their float-point
on the air, soppy earths, all this
in the then beloved's gaze,
the ball in the socket at the top of his thighbone
like a marrow eye through which the foreshore could have
seen us, his hip joints like the gravital centres
of my spirit. Then we'd lie, feet toward the Atlantic,
my hypothermic claw tucked
beneath the heat of his flank, under
day moon, or coming storm,
swallow, heron, prism-bow, drizzle,

osprey, test-pilot out to No Man's.
And then, before our sight, the half world
folded on itself, and bent, and swallowed,
and opened, again, its wet, long
mouths, and drank itself.

SLOWLY HE STARTS

And slowly he starts to seem more far
away, he seems to waft, drift
at a distance, once-husband in his grey suit
with the shimmer to its weave – his hands at his sides,
as if on damselfly wings he seems
to be borne through the air past my window. And a breeze
takes him, up and about, he is like
a Chagall bridegroom, without the faith-
fulness, or with a faithfulness which can
change brides once, he is carried, on a current,
like a creature of a slightly other species,
speech unwoken, in him, as yet,
and without the weight to hold him to
the ground. Silent meteor,
summer shower of perseids,
he is floated here and there so dim and
quiet he is like a sleeper, with large,
heavy-lidded, calm eyes
open. I am glad not to have lost him
entirely, but to see him moved
at the whim of the sky, like a man in the wind,
drawn as if on a barge resting on
updrafts, mild downdrops, he is like
an icon, he is like a fantasy.
I did not know him, I knew my idea
of him. The first years alone,
they said I would get over him
sometime soon, and the skin of my heart
seemed to be lying along the skin
of some naked heart. But now the invisible
streams show themselves, in their motions
of him, in the low empyrean
above the playground – look, he is out
there, casting his narrow shadow

over the faces in the carriages
in the park, and I am in here! I do not let
go of him yet, but hold the string
and watch my idea of him pull away
and stay, and pull away, my silver kite.

RED SEA

And at a party, or in any crowd, years
after he has left, there will come an almost
visible image of my ex, appearing
at the far side of a room, moving
toward me, making his way between people,
as the soul used to make its way, through
clothes, until it lay, bare,
beside the soul of the beloved, then they seemed
to swim into each other, and they sang. Before me,
on either side, facing each other
like opposing armies, two columns
of words keen and catcall to each other:

relinquishment,	fastening,
abjure,	trice up;
forfeiture,	colligate,
disclaim,	padlock;
free,	ligate,
abandon,	yoke,
desert,	surcingle,
secede,	belay;
quit,	solder,
yield,	snood,
leave,	enchain,
release,	bind;
	clinch,
	latchet,
	suture,
	peg;
	splice,
	wattle,
	harness,
	nail,

much work to be done. And Love said, to me,

What if I, myself, asked you
to love him less. And I stepped out into
the trough between the pillars, the dry
ground through the midst of the sea – the waters
a wall unto me, on the right hand,
and on the left.

RUNNING INTO YOU

Seeing you again, after so long,
seeing you with her, and actually almost
not wanting you back,
doesn't seem to make me feel separate from you. But you
      seemed
covered with her, like a child working with glue
who's young to be working with glue. 'If I could
choose, a place to die',
it would never have been in your arms, old darling,
we figured I'd see you out, in mine,
it was never in doubt that you had suffered more than I
when young. That moved me so much about you,
the way you were a dumbstruck one
and yet you seemed to know everything
I did not know, which was everything
except the gift of gab — and oh well
dirty dancing and how to apologise.
When I went up to you two, at the art opening,
I felt I had nothing to apologise for,
I felt like a somewhat buoyant creature
with feet of I don't know what, recovered-from sorrow,
which held me nicely to the gallery floor as to the
surface of a planet, some lunar orb
once part of the earth.

I'D ASK HIM FOR IT

Rarely, he would sing to me,
I don't know what scale he used, maybe Arab,
seventeen steps to the octave, or Chinese,
five. It was microtonal, a-
harmonic, its staff was of the bass clef,
but I don't know how far below baritone
it went, C below middle C or
lower, down into those mineral regions – I would
ask it of him directly, I would be
lying along him, and would say to him,
softly, confiding, 'Do me some low notes', and he'd
open his wide, thin-lipped, tone-deaf
mouth, and seek down, for a breath
near the early deposited shales,
he would make the male soundings, and if I had been
finishing I would again, central
level bubble of a whole note slowly
bursting. I think he loved being loved,
I think those were the cadences,
plagal, of a good, lived life.
He liked it a long time, tonic,
dominant, subdominant, and now
I want to relearn the intervals, to
journey with a man among the thirds and fifths,
augmented, diminished, with a light touch,
sforzando, rallentando, agitato, the usual
adores and dotes – and of course what I really
want is some low notes.

THE SHORE

And when I was nearing the ocean, for the first
time since we'd parted –
approaching that place where the liquid stillborn
robe pulls along pulverised boulder –
that month, each year, came back, when we'd swim,
first thing, then go back to bed, to the kelp-field, our
green hair pouring into each other's green
hair of skull and crux bone. We were like
a shore, I thought – two elements, touching
each other, dozing in the faith that we were
knowing each other, one of us
maybe a little too much a hunter,
the other a little too polar of affection,
polar of summer mysteriousness,
magnetic in reticent mourning. His first
mate was a husky pup, who died,
from the smoke, in a fire. Someone asked him,
once, to think from the point of view
of the flames, and his face relaxed, and he said,
Delicious. I hope he can come to think
of me like that. The weeks before he left,
I'd lie on him, as if not heavy,
for a minute, after the last ferocious
ends of the world, as if loneliness had come
overland to its foreshore, breaker,
shelf, trench, and then had fallen down to where
it seemed it could not be recovered from. Elements,
protect him, and those we love, whether we both
love them or not. Physics, author of our
death, stand by us. Compass, we are sinking
down through sea-purse toward eyes on stalks.
We have always been going back, since birth,
back toward not being alive. Doing it –
it – with him, I felt I shared

a dignity, an inhuman sweetness
of his sisters and brothers the iceberg calf,
the snow ant, the lighthouse rook,
the albatross, who once it breaks out of the
shell, and rises, does not set down again.

POEM OF THANKS

Years later, long single,
I want to turn to his departed back,
and say, What gifts we had of each other!
What pleasure – confiding, open-eyed,
fainting with what we were allowed to stay up
late doing. And you couldn't say,
could you, that the touch you had from me
was other than the touch of one
who could love for life – whether we were suited
or not – for *life,* like a sentence. And now that I
consider, the touch that I had from you
became not the touch of the long view, but like the
tolerant willingness of one
who is passing through. Colleague of sand
by moonlight – and by beach noonlight, once,
and of straw, salt bale in a barn, and mulch
inside a garden, between the rows – once-
partner of up against the wall in that tiny
bathroom with the lock that fluttered like a chrome
butterfly beside us, hip-height, the familiar
of our innocence, which was the ignorance
of what would be asked, what was required,
thank you for every hour. And I
accept your thanks, as if it were
a gift of yours, to give them – let's part
equals, as we were in every bed, pure
equals of the earth.

LEFT-WIFE BOP

Suddenly, I remember the bar
of gold my young husband bought
and buried somewhere near our farmhouse. During our
divorce – as much ours as any
Sunday dinner was, or what was
called the nap which followed it –
he wanted to go to the house, one last
time. *Please, not with her,*
please, and he said, *All right,* and I don't know
why, when I figured it out, later,
that he'd gone to dig up our bar of gold,
I didn't mind. I think it is because of how
even it was, between us, how even
we divided the chores, though he was the greater
wage-earner, how evenly
the bounty of pleasure fell between us –
wait, what's a bounty? Like a kidnap fee?
He fell in love with her because I
didn't suit him anymore –
nor him, me, though I could not see it, but he
saw it for me. Even, even,
our playing field – we inspired in each other
a generousness. And he did not give
his secrets to his patients, but I gave my secrets
to you, dear strangers, and his, too –
unlike the warbling of coming, I sang
for two. Uneven, uneven, our scales
of contentment went slowly askew, and when he
hopped off, on the ground floor, and I
sailed through the air, poetic justice
was done. So when I think of him
going with his pick and shovel to exactly where he
knew the ingot was, and working his
way down, until the air

touched it and released its light,
I think he was doing what I'd been doing, but I'd
got a little ahead of him – he was
redressing the balance, he was leading his own life.

YEARS LATER

At first glance, there on the bench
where he'd agreed to meet, it didn't seem to be
him – but then the face of grim
friendliness was my former husband's,
like the face of a creature looking out
from inside its Knox. No fault, no knock,
clever nut of the hearing aid
hidden in the ear I do not feel I
love, anymore, patch of bandage on the cheek
peopled with tiny lichen from a land I don't
know. We walk. I had not remembered
how deep he held himself inside
himself – my fun, for thirty-two years,
to lure him out. I still kind of want to,
as if I see him as a being with a baby-paw
caught. His voice is the same – low,
still pushed around the level-bubble
in his throat. We talk of the kids, and it's
as if that will never be taken from us.
But it feels as if he's not here –
though he's here, it feels as if, for me,
there's no one there – as when he was with me
it seemed there was no one there for any other
woman. For the first thirty years. Now I see
I've been hoping, each time we meet, that he would praise me
for how well I took it, but it's not to be.
Are you happy as you thought you'd be,
I ask. Yes. And his smile is touchingly
pleased. *I thought you'd look happier,*
I say, *but after all, when I am
looking at you, you're with me!* We smile.
His eyes warm, a moment, with the accustomed
shift, as if he's turning into
the species he was for those thirty years.

And turning back. I glance toward his torso
once, his legs – he's like a stick figure,
now, the way, when I was with him, other
men seemed like Ken dolls, all clothes. Even
the gold of his fresh wedding ring is no
blade to my rib – this is Married Ken. As I
walk him toward his street I joke, and for an instant
he's alive toward me, a gem of sea of
pond in his eye. Then that retreat into himself,
which always moved me, as if there were
a sideways gravity, in him, toward some
vanishing point. And no, he does not
want to meet again, in a year – when we
part, it is with a dry bow
and Good-bye. And then there is the spring park,
damp as if freshly peeled, sweet
greenhouse, green cemetery with no
dead in it – except, in some shaded
woods, under some years of leaves and
rotted cones, the body of a warbler
like a whole note fallen from the sky – my old
love for him, like a songbird's rib cage picked clean.

SEPTEMBER 2001, NEW YORK CITY

A week later, I said to a friend: I don't
think I could ever write about it.
Maybe in a year I could write something.
There is something in me maybe someday
to be written; now it is folded, and folded,
and folded, like a note in school. And in my dream
someone was playing jacks, and in the air there was a
huge, thrown, tilted jack
on fire. And when I woke up, I found myself
counting the days since I had last seen
my ex-husband – only two years, and some weeks
and hours. We had signed the papers and come down to the
ground floor of the Chrysler Building,
the intact beauty of its lobby around us
like a king's tomb, on the ceiling the little
painted plane, in the mural, flying. And it
entered my strictured heart, this morning,
slightly, shyly as if warily,
untamed, a greater sense of the sweetness
and plenty of his ongoing life,
unknown to me, unseen by me,
unheard by me, untouched by me,
but known by others, seen by others,
heard, touched. And it came to me,
for moments at a time, moment after moment,
to be glad for him that he is with the one
he feels was meant for him. And I thought of my
mother, minutes from her death, eighty-five
years from her birth, the almost warbler
bones of her shoulder under my hand, the
eggshell skull, as she lay in some peace
in the clean sheets, and I could tell her the best

of my poor, partial love, I could sing her
out, with it, I saw the luck
and the luxury of that hour.

WHAT LEFT?

Something like a half-person
left my young husband's body,
and something like the other half
left my ovary. Later,
the new being, complete, slowly
left my body. And a portion of breath
left the air of the delivery room,
entering the little mouth,
and the milk left the breast, and went
into the fat cuffs of the wrists.
Years later, during his cremation,
the liquids left my father's corpse,
and the smoke left the flue. And even
later, my mother's ashes left
my hand, and fell as seethe into the salt
chop. My then husband made
a self, a life, I made beside him
a self, a life, gestation. We grew
strong, in direction. We clarified
in vision, we deepened in our silence and our speaking.
We did not hold still, we moved, we are moving
still – we made, with each other, a moving
like a kind of music: duet; then solo,
solo. We fulfilled something in each other –
I believed in him, he believed in me, then we
grew, and grew, I grieved him, he grieved me,
I completed with him, he completed with me, we
made whole cloth together, we succeeded,
we perfected what lay between him and me,
I did not deceive him, he did not deceive me,
I did not leave him, he did not leave me,
I freed him, he freed me.

ACKNOWLEDGEMENTS

Acknowledgements are due to the editors of the following:

American Poetry Review, *Atlantic Monthly*, *Brick*, *Five Points*, *Green Mountain Review*, *Gulf Coast*, *New Yorker*, *Ontario Review*, *Ploughshares*, *Poetry*, *Poetry London*, *Slate*, *Southern Review*, *Threepenny Review*, *Tin House*, *Tracking the Storm*, *TriQuarterly*